WELCO

TO WORSHIP IN THE WILDERNESS

We are so glad that you have chosen to join us on this journey! Whether you are coming as an individual, part of a group, or as a whole church following our Sunday resources, we are really pleased to be on this Lent pilgrimage with you.

First, a random fact: did you know that a dead tree trunk lying in a forest has more life living within it than a live tree?

Nature reinforces what the Bible tries to show us over and over again: the way to life comes through death. Resurrection follows crucifixion. Transformation comes through the dry, lifeless path of the wilderness.

We all like the idea of being changed, but are we willing to take the wilderness path? The good news is, Jesus has already been there. He wants to take us by the hand, and lead us in the way of abundant, everlasting life.

Wilderness in the Bible

Countless characters in the Old Testament including Jacob, Hagar, Job, David and Elijah met with God in the wilderness. The people of Israel experienced their most defining period as they escaped from Egypt and then wandered for 40 years, learning to trust God and worship him in that arid, threatening place.

Centuries later, Jesus himself walked the wilderness path for 40 days. He chose obedience where his people failed. He knew our temptations, our sorrows, our struggles - in fact, he took them on his shoulders and died for them. So we are not alone on our journey. Jesus walks with us.

Wilderness in our lives

We might not live in a desert, but we know what wilderness feels like. It might be that our jobs, homes or communities feel like a place of barren exile. We can experience the wilderness of losing a loved one, being fired or getting ill. Or it might be that our inner worlds are the desert places, as we go through periods of feeling dry, doubtful or depressed. Songwriter Michael Card writes:

> "The wilderness is still the place of worship. But for you and me it is not a matter of dunes and dry ground; in fact, it may be deceptively green. Our hunger and thirst are more spiritual realities than physical ones... Our deep need for Living Water is just as intense as any thirst their parched throats ever knew."
>
> Michael Card, A Sacred Sorrow, page 24.

Wilderness worship

The aim of this book is to understand God's heart for us in the wilderness. We will explore stories from across the Bible which touch on desert experiences. We will unpack wilderness worship practices, such as simplicity, solitude and silence. We will wrestle with the difficult emotions which arise in our desert journeys. And we will look to the hope that we have in our "Man of Sorrows" - Jesus.

To help you engage in varied ways we have included things like reflection questions with space to scribble your responses, ideas for creative interaction, and practical steps to walk out the teaching in everyday life. It may be that you hoped just to sit and read a book with no consequences - if so, sorry about that!

Joking aside, we would encourage

you to hold a balance between knowing what works for you, and also occasionally taking a risk. Why not give something a try which would not usually be part of your "quiet time" or prayer life? There is no compulsion to do anything, but we have worked hard to include activities we feel will be life-giving and transformative.

How the weeks work

In general, there is a reflection for each weekday of Lent. We think it is realistic that weekends might be busy, or they might be a good time to catch up on a day you missed during the week.

The first section follows Ash Wednesday, so there are only two reflections for that week. We have left the final week after Palm Sunday free (except for some final review questions) so that you can follow your usual pattern of engaging with Holy Week.

If your church is following our Sunday material, you should find that the weekly reflections unpack and complement this. If you want to engage as a small group, you can easily adapt the questions and responses to fit group discussion.

Sam and Sara

Ash Wednesday

A SECRET JOURNEY

"Don't tear your clothing in your grief, but tear your hearts instead."
(Joel 2:13, NLT)

0.1 - SECRETS IN A TIME OF OVER-SHARING

"your Father, who sees what is done in secret, will reward you" (Matthew 6:4, 6, 18)

Read: Matthew 6:1-6, 16-18

"Revealed: Government minister's secret love child!"
"Corporation hides funds in secret off-shore account!"

It is not unusual to feel that we are bombarded with these kinds of headlines. Newspapers and websites hope to cash in on our natural curiosity around secrets. Very rarely do the headlines cry out: "Revealed: Government minister's secret habit of taking out neighbour's trash!" or "Corporation secretly invests funds in homeless shelter!" No, you can be sure that those kinds of things will not remain secret for very long.

Jesus' encouragements to us in Matthew 6 are so counter-cultural that they almost read like a joke, and it was the same in his own time. This passage is not only advice for engaging in spiritual practices, but perhaps also a critique of those who do it for their own gain. Jesus will have witnessed those individuals who arrived at the synagogue to give money to the poor, accompanied by announcements of their intentions. He claimed that these people had received their reward for doing good things already, as they were now honoured by the people around them.

Reflect: Are there things that you do in order to impress other people? What areas are you most tempted to do this in - your work, family life, finances, good deeds, spiritual life, or some other sphere?

In the same way, the spiritual practice of fasting is not intended to be to impress others, but to seek God and to go deeper in prayer. Looking "sombre" and "disfiguring" yourself in public may not be so different to today's Christian posting their spiritual activities on Facebook or Twitter for all to see.

At the start of this journey of "Worship in the Wilderness" you may want to search your own motives: are you engaging with a Lent series because you want to draw nearer to God? Or because a leader told you to? Or because your small group will be impressed? James writes:

> "Come near to God and he will come near to you. Wash your hands, you sinners, and purify your hearts, you double-minded. Grieve, mourn and wail. Change your laughter to mourning and your joy to gloom. Humble yourselves before the Lord, and he will lift you up." (James 4:8-10)

Confess: Use this space to ask God's forgiveness where your motives have been wrong. Then take a quiet moment to receive God's acceptance afresh, knowing that he will "come near to you" and "lift you up".

Pray: Make this prayer your own:

Father, you promise to reward what is done for you in secret.
Your rewards are far greater than money, fame or fortune.
You reward us with a transformed heart,
contentment in every circumstance,
and an eternal relationship with you.
Help me to seek you quietly, unobtrusively,
and with all my heart. Amen.

0.2 - TORN HEARTS AND MOURNING

"Rend your heart and not your garments."
(Joel 2:13)

Read: Joel 2:1-2, 12-17

Tearing your clothes is an ancient Jewish practice for times of mourning. Even today, Jews engage in *keriah*, the Hebrew verb for "rip" or "rend". Although a very dramatic event in the Old Testament (for example, Jacob tearing his clothes upon being told of Joseph's violent death in Genesis 37), today's *keriah* is regulated by rules around who needs to tear what in their funeral clothes, how big the tear should be and when the tear is allowed to be mended. A spontaneous expression of grief has been packaged neatly into a box of rules.

Every faith or culture will have customs and rules surrounding mourning. Black used to be the colour of choice for funeral services, signifying the seriousness, respect and sobriety of the occasion. This rule has been softened somewhat, as black becomes the go-to colour for rock stars, fashion designers and intense teenagers alike. Yet most of us would still think seriously about what to wear for a funeral, foregoing the sequinned party dress for something more discreet.

It is interesting to think about mourning in the context of prayer and spirituality. The prophet Joel encourages the people of Israel to engage with practices usually associated with funerals or wakes, but to use them in the context of drawing near to God.

Reflect: Do you have experiences of mourning? How do you feel about expressing grief before God?

As Christians in the time after Jesus we might think that we do not have to bother with awe and trembling any more. The writer to the Hebrews, however, reminds us that even as Christians we are to "worship God acceptably with reverence and awe, for our 'God is a consuming fire.'" (Heb. 12:28-29) Let us try to shake off our over-familiarity with this holy, awe-inspiring, righteous God, and linger for a while in the picture which Joel presents to us:

> "Let all who live in the land tremble, for the day of the Lord is coming" (v. 1)
> "'Even now,' declares the Lord, 'return to me with all your heart, with fasting and weeping and mourning.'" (v. 12)
> "Rend your heart and not your garments." (v. 13)

In most of our contemporary worship we celebrate, sing joyful songs and greet one another with a smile and a hope for peace. But, before a holy, righteous God, ought we to sometimes come in weeping and mourning? For example, when we consider our own role in the textile trade, requiring sweatshop workers in Bangladesh to live inhuman lifestyles, perhaps weeping is the appropriate response? When the nation we live in sells weapon to other nations, which use them to oppress the poor, ought we to come before God in mourning? And we will all know the pride, the selfishness and the secret sins which dirty our own hearts and cause God pain.

The ash of Ash Wednesday signifies the truth that we will all one day return to dust (see Genesis 3:19) and is a call for us to repent while there is still time. Joel reminds us that, rather than a big show of repentance, God wants the true repentance of our hearts. Use the space to the right to reflect on your own heart: is there anything there which requires a mournful repentance?

Pray: Write or draw your prayer in this ash:

First Week

A SPIRIT-LED JOURNEY

"Let my people go that they may
worship me in the wilderness"
(Exodus 7:16)

1.1 - LED BY THE SPIRIT

"... the Spirit sent him out into the wilderness" (Mark 1:12)

Read: Mark 1:9-13

Reflect: What comes to your mind when you hear the phrase "led by the Holy Spirit"? In this passage the Holy Spirit descends upon Jesus and then immediately leads him. But where does it lead him to? What were the consequences of this guidance?

Draw: Consider the ways God has led you in your life. Draw a graph of your life below, noting the highs, lows and other important events.

Positive times

Your birth

today

Difficult times

Now reflect on the following questions:

• Have there been times in your life where you have clearly sensed God guiding you? Perhaps mark these on your timeline.

• Are there times you can look back at now and realise that God was leading you, even though you did not know it at the time? Mark those on the timeline too.

• Prayerfully consider those times that do not seem positive. There might be times when you felt you followed God's lead but it did not work out the way you expected. Be honest about how you feel, and allow space to listen to God. Reflect on what it means that the Spirit led Jesus into the wilderness.

1.2 - WORSHIP IN THE WILDERNESS

"Let my people go, so that they may worship me in the wilderness." (Exodus 7:16)

Read: Exodus 15:22-27

How would you rate your church's Sunday worship? Do you love the music in your services, the ways people pray and celebrate communion, the attempts at creativity, testimony and reflection? Perhaps if you are honest, sometimes you struggle, disagree with the way things are presented, or find yourself thinking "I would be able to worship far better if they led the worship the way I like it!"

It is easy to think that we will worship better if we have more - better music, a more spiritual pastor, a louder PA system, a newer projector screen. Or perhaps you lament the loss of older forms of worship - the hymns or prayer book you were so familiar with, the quiet reflection you used to experience. None of these things are bad in and of themselves. In fact they are all gifts from God. But if we depend on them to make our worship happen we're going to be in for a surprise.

Reflect: Are there some things you rely on before you will worship?

God told Moses in Exodus 7 to demand of Pharaoh that the people of Israel may be set free to go and worship in the wilderness. He wanted to teach them to worship, not by adding more, but by taking things away. In the wilderness they could rely on nothing other than his presence with them. Songwriter Michael Card has reflected:

"True worship begins in the wilderness. Praise is almost always the answer to a plea that arises in the desert... In the wilderness the children of Israel discovered that above all others, He was worthy. He was the Father they wanted. He was the Provider they needed." Michael Card, *A Sacred Sorrow*, pages 23-24.

Is there a desert in your life? Perhaps your church services have felt dry or difficult for you. Maybe your family or relationships are seeming like a bit of a wilderness, or your work life is a barren place right now. It could be that all the outer things are fine, but inside, in your spirit, you are going through a wasteland, a "dark night of the soul".

Reflect: Note down any situations which feel like a wilderness to you at the moment.

_____

_____

_____

_____

_____

_____

The good news is this: God has not abandoned you in the wilderness. In fact, he allows his people to go through times of dryness so that they will see that it is he who provides and be more aware of his presence. He wants you to call out to him in the wilderness so that he might provide the water of life you need, and so that you might worship him from your heart.

Rest: Take a moment in quiet to acknowledge God's presence with you.

1.3 - DID MY AMAZING HANDS ACHIEVE THIS?

"The Lord your God led you all the way in the wilderness these forty years" (Deuteronomy 8:2)

Read: Deuteronomy 8:1-18

The current Children's Bible we are reading as a family presents the story of the Israelite Exodus from Egypt in quite a lot of detail. Because we have read this story many times before, our children know what is coming. The first time Israel starts whining about something, our daughter will say something like: "Oh, here we go again...!" And when God answers their prayer, and the people of Israel respond with a promise to always trust God in the future, she will quip: "Yeah, whatever..." It becomes an ongoing joke as we read the story; the tragic comedy of Israel forgetting to remember.

The beginning of Deuteronomy reads a bit like a "director's commentary" of the grand events of the Exodus. Some of the same stories are revisited, but with added insights into what was really going on, and how Israel's engagement with God impacted the events. Chapter 8 is the reminder to God's people to remember, detailing all the ways in which the Lord provided for them in the wilderness:

> "Remember how the Lord your God led you all the way in the desert these forty years..." (v.2)
> "Be careful that you do not forget the Lord your God..." (v.10)
> "But remember the Lord your God..." (v.18)
> "If you ever forget the Lord your God... you will surely be destroyed." (v.19)

Why all these reminders to remember? What was the purpose of forty long years of wandering in the wilderness? Some people estimate that the journey should, under ordinary circumstances, have taken less than two weeks. So why forty years?!

The comedy repetitions of the people whining, and then trusting again, and then whining all over again, as well as Moses having to tell them repeatedly to remember, should give us a clue. The Israelite people were very forgetful - much like the rest of us.

If you do not remember the Lord, Moses tells the Israelites, you may start thinking that this was all your doing. You will become proud and think that you have earned all these good things. "You may say to yourself, 'My power and the strength of my hands have produced this wealth for me.'" (v. 17)

Sometimes God leads us into the wilderness, because that is what it takes to turn from worshipping ourselves to worshipping God. It's in the easy times we start believing our own press: "yeah, I am pretty amazing" or "look at this fantastic thing I achieved." And we too, like the Israelites, are guilty of forgetting the source of all goodness. In the wilderness, however, when all the external aids and props are laid down, we have space to remember and turn to the God who gave us life.

Reflect: What things in your life are you tempted to take the credit for, when you know that the glory really should go to God? Note these below.

Pray: Make this prayer your own:

Heavenly Father, everything I have comes from you.
All my achievements, relationships and possessions
are the fruit of your goodness to me.
As I journey through the wilderness with you
make me more aware of my dependence.
Help me to learn trust, grow humility,
and give me a thankful
and generous heart.
In the name of Jesus
I pray, amen.

1.4 - FEEDING ON JESUS

"Jesus declared 'I am the bread of life. Whoever comes to me will never go hungry'" (John 6:35)

Read: John 6:25-35

Food that never runs out is the stuff of fairytales, like the story of *The Magic Porridge Pot* by the Brothers Grimm. You can see the attraction of these stories in Medieval Europe. Children who never had the abundance that we live with today, listening to these tales with big, wide eyes. A porridge pot that never runs out? Enough for everyone to eat until they are full? What a marvellous thing!

The people in first century Palestine were not so different. Like most people groups in human history, their lives were centred around growing food, collecting wood to cook food, gathering food, hunting for food, trading for food. It is only recently that there has been more than enough food around (at least for some of us), making it unusual to spend long days working for and worrying about food.

It seems like the people listening to Jesus were harking back to the amazing stories of the Exodus, marvelling at the idea of God providing *manna* in the desert. Enough food for everyone, provided straight from the hand of God, and they only needed to collect it (see Exodus 16).

Reflect: You may not struggle to find food, but what daily, basic needs do you rely on God for? Make a list and take a moment to be thankful, or ask God to provide where you are currently lacking.

It almost seems like Jesus is leading the crowd on in this story, making use of their desire for food and pulling them in with his talk of bread. These days someone might make a claim to the Advertising Standards Authority for "false advertising". Yes, he is talking about bread, but no, you will not technically be able to eat it.

Jesus is talking about something more important than a mere loaf of wholemeal. He is talking about the very epicentre of life itself - he is talking about *himself*. Do not rely on food, do not rely on stuff, do not rely on your own hands, he says. Rely on the Bread of Life and you will never hunger, nor thirst, again.

Write on the bread roll below what it is in life that you desire, which hungers you may need to bring to Jesus for recalibration. Ask for forgiveness where you have worried about the less important things in life.

Pray: Make this prayer your own:

Lord Jesus, you are the Bread of Life.
I choose to turn to you today,
to leave my worries and my desires for what is not you.
Feed my soul and spirit, that I may be satisfied.
Amen.

1.5 - LIKE A BIRD IN THE DESERT

"He will respond to the prayer of the destitute; he will not despise their plea." (Psalm 102:17)

Read: Psalm 102:1-11 slowly and reflectively.

Verses 3-11, especially, contain many vivid images: smoke, glowing embers, withered grass, desert owls, ash, evening shadows and so on. Which image stands out to you? Draw something to show that on the image below, even if it is just something symbolic, or write the words which sum up the thing that strikes you.

Reflect: Look at the image you have picked out. Think of adjectives to describe this image, and the emotions that the image awakes in you. Scribble these around your image or word. Does the image reflect any of your own life experience, or that of someone near to you? If so, how?

Read: Psalm 102:17-20. These speak about the response of God to those crying out to him. Rewrite these verses in your own words to form either a prayer or a word of blessing over yourself or someone else who is suffering.

_____

_____

_____

_____

Do you know someone else who might need to hear this blessing? Consider writing these words to them in a text message or on a card today, as an encouragement.

Second Week

A SIMPLE JOURNEY

"... the rich simplicity of
being yourself before God."
(1 Timothy 6:6, MSG)

2.1 - SIMPLICITY: FREEDOM FROM NOISE

"... the Lord was not in the fire. And after the fire came a gentle whisper." (1 Kings 19:12)

Read: 1 Kings 19:1-13

We live in a noisy world. There are more opportunities than ever to avoid any potential silence in our lives. TV, radio, podcasts and music - many of us fill our days going from one noise to the next. Then there are the noises we do not choose: the person on the bus playing tinny music on their mobile phone, the piped music in every shop and restaurant and (if we live in an urban setting) the constant cars, sirens and aeroplanes.

Although we cannot say for certain what Elijah's expectations were when he arrived at Mount Horeb, reading between the lines it seems had thought God might appear in thunder and lightning. And why would he not? Elijah knew about Moses' encounter with God and the flames of fire from within a bush (Ex. 3:2); he knew about God leading the Israelites through the wilderness with the dramatic pillars of fire and cloud (Ex. 13: 21). Indeed, only a short time before, God had done something dramatic in Elijah's life: lighting up the water-soaked wood and animal sacrifice in a glorious blaze in full view of the people and the false prophets (1 Kgs. 18).

And yet, when the Lord passes by Elijah, he does not appear in the powerful wind, the earthquake or the fire. God's presence is revealed in a "gentle whisper", or a "still small voice". Or one translation prefers "the sound of sheer silence" (NRSV).

Imagine: What would it be like to hear "the sound of sheer silence"?

Many of us come from church traditions where the loud and dramatic are signifiers of God's presence, whether that be through large choirs, thundering organs or wailing electric guitars. The crowd raise their voices, the chorus reverberates from the congregation, the drums resound. Perhaps we, like Elijah, need to change our expectations? Perhaps we need to contemplate the possibility that God will be present with us in our quiet, humble prayer times, just as much as when we are engaged in festival worship?

To worship in the wilderness is by nature a quiet and secluded event. Here we do not find the roaring crowds but instead the silent, solitary heart seeking the Lord. Here is not the loud organ or the well-rehearsed band, but the individual humbly coming before God with no noise behind which to hide.

Challenge: experiment with spending increasingly long times in silence, a bit like when you train for a running race. Have no agenda other than sitting quietly in God's presence. Start with a very short time and build up to a longer five minutes or so. Afterwards, record what you feel during these times, and what you are learning. Put a bookmark on this page and return to the challenge in your own time during this period of Lent.

30 sec silence	Date/Time:	Notes:
1 min silence	Date/Time:	Notes:
2 mins silence	Date/Time:	Notes:
3 mins silence	Date/Time:	Notes:
4 mins silence	Date/Time:	Notes:
5 mins silence	Date/Time:	Notes:

2.2 - SIMPLICITY: FREEDOM FROM SPEAKING

"Be still, and know that I am God" (Psalm 46:10)

In the last devotion we explored the idea that God may meet us in the silence, as he did with Elijah. But there is another angle to silence, that of refraining from speaking. Henri Nouwen in his book on the Desert Mothers and Fathers spoke of silence as a way of guarding the fire of the Holy Spirit in us. He wrote:

> "Sometimes it seems that our many words are more an expression of our doubt than our faith. It is as if we are not sure that God's Spirit can touch the hearts of people: we have to help him out and, with many words, convince others of his power. But it is precisely this wordy unbelief that quenches the fire." Henri Nouwen, *The Way of the Heart*, page 54.

Psalm 46:10 seems to connect our stillness with our God-awareness: when we quieten ourselves we can attend to God and know who he is. There is humility in silence, an acknowledgement that perhaps the words I have to say may not be all that important in the greater scheme of things. This humility is encapsulated in the famous verse from Ecclesiastes, wisdom literature for the ancient times as much as for our own:

> "Do not be quick with your mouth,
> do not be hasty in your heart to utter anything before God.
> God is in heaven and you are on earth, so let your words be few."
> (Ecc. 5:2)

Practical steps: Here are a few ideas for working out these principles today:

- When you pray, consider using more silence than words.
- Create some time for solitude - a walk alone, shutting yourself in a room, or a longer retreat.
- When you are with other people, be conscious of listening more than you speak. Ask them questions, show that you are interested in what they have to say, and don't be afraid to leave silences. Notice how this changes your conversations and interactions.

2.3 - SIMPLICITY: SIMPLE PRAYER

"God, have mercy on me, a sinner." (Luke 18:13)

Read: Luke 18:9-14

Jesus teaches that it is the attitude in which we come to him that matters, not our outward showings of righteousness or spirituality. Centring Prayer is one way of simplifying the manner in which we pray. It helps us to rely less on eloquent words, or getting through our list of prayer points.

Centring Prayer involves choosing an anchor word or phrase. Perhaps this could be a name of God, a characteristic of him, or a phrase like the prayer of the tax collector in Jesus' story. The idea is to speak or think this anchor as you come into God's presence, with no other agenda than to be with him. If you feel yourself distracted by something or your thoughts wander, recognise this and then turn back to your anchor.

We encourage you to try Centring Prayer today as a way of praying simply. Choose your anchor word, and repeat it as you sit in God's presence. If it helps you to visualise things, you can use the space below to write your anchor in the circle and then make note of your distractions on the periphery before pointing yourself back to God.

2.4 - SIMPLICITY: FREEDOM FROM DISTRACTIONS

"While they were worshipping the Lord and fasting..." (Acts 13:2)

Read: Acts 13:1-3, 14:21-23

What distracts you when you try to pray? This morning, halfway through my Bible reading, I (Sara) realised that I had drifted off for a full five minutes thinking about an old acquaintance whose picture had popped up on Facebook the evening before. Now perhaps I should have paused my reading and prayed for this person. But there is also something about removing distractions in our lives to help us seek God in a more focused way.

The Old Testament has much to say about fasting. The only day the Lord commanded his people to spend fasting was the Day of Atonement, a holy and special day of seeking God's forgiveness. But there were also voluntary times in the Old Testament, where God's people fasted as they repented, or sought God's attention for particular issues.

In the New Testament, Jesus himself and the leaders of the first church fasted, but the advice is much less prescriptive. We have already read Jesus' command to secrecy - when you fast, do not show off about it. Beyond that, there is little in the way of practical advice to be found. The focus is more on the heart than the acts themselves. Food is presented as a spiritually neutral matter (see for example Col. 2:16-17, 20-23 and 1 Cor. 8:8). The way to the Father is through Christ, not through skipping meals.

Reflect: How have you experienced fasting in the past? Has it ever been a source of guilt, or trying to force God to do something for you? Talk to him about this.

Among other reasons to fast, the issue of distraction is worth bringing up in this context. In our passages from Acts today we see the early church leaders seeking God concerning serious matters. Who would be sent out as a missionary? Who would lead this newly planted church? In those decisions, there is a need for focus and attention to the Lord's voice. Fasting would have removed the distractions of meal times and prolonged the time of prayer. You have to remember that life 2000 years ago did not involve three minute microwave meals. For many, their whole day was taken up with gathering, trading, preparing and cooking the meals, as well as cleaning and clearing up afterwards. Fasting released extra time to seek God.

Practical steps: What distracts you from coming to God? What can you do this week, or this period of Lent, to reduce the amount of distractions encroaching on your life with God?

- Cutting down internet or smartphone use.
- Switching off the TV more often.
- Choosing simple food requiring less time in the kitchen.
- Skipping some meals to take time to pray.
- Taking more walks instead of driving.

Fasting is also a physical reminder of our need to trust in God. We have seen this when thinking about the Israelites in the wilderness, and when Jesus resists the devil by reminding him that "man shall not live on bread alone" (Luke 5:4). Saying "no" to one thing - even a good thing like food, technology, social interactions and possessions - is a way of saying "yes" to the deeper satisfaction of knowing God and trusting in his provision. It equips us to live with healthier attitudes towards these things.

Pray: Make this prayer your own:

*Jesus, teach me to occasionally live with less,
to fast those things which distract me
or in which I am tempted to put my trust.
I know that you have the best for me and are leading me
in the way of everlasting, abundant life. Amen.*

2.5 - SIMPLICITY: FREEDOM FROM STUFF

"Do not take a purse or bag or sandals"
(Luke 10:4)

Read: Luke 10:1-7

If you were to pit an army of lambs against an army of wolves in some strange imaginary scenario, what precautions would you take? Well, the little baby sheep are not as fast as the wolves, so they would need some sort of speedy transport. The sharp wolf teeth would be an issue, so we might want to kit the lambs out with full body armour. And, as lambs have no strength or powers to help them in attack, they would definitely need the most efficient types of weaponry.

Sending the lambs towards the wolves with no equipment at all seems unkind, to say the least. This, however, seems to be what Jesus is doing here. He is sending a large group of disciples out as missionaries, likening them to lambs being sent among wolves. But he is sending them without any special equipment - any "stuff". "Do not take a purse or bag or sandals..." he says in verse 4.

If I were a lamb encountering the big, bad wolf, it would be comforting to have a purse with me to either try to pay the wolf off, or to pay someone stronger to chase it away! At the very least, a good pair of sandals in which to run for my life would be very useful. But Jesus wants these particular lambs of his to go, trusting in him alone.

I wonder how much of our own stuff we consider essential equipment? We are perhaps prudent and save for a rainy day, hoping to stave off evil using money more than the name of Jesus. Or maybe we spend a lot of money on clothes to look the part, believing that our outfit will protect us from attack. It could be that our insurance policies or our expensive educations are the things we defend ourselves with. Or perhaps your home is your "castle"?

Reflect: What things do you use to protect yourself? What are the things that you believe you need, things which hinder you from trusting in Christ alone?

When the disciples return, it seems that despite their lack of provisions they had everything they needed in Christ. They "returned with joy and said: 'Lord, even the demons submit to us in your name.'" (10:17) They didn't need money to pay off evil. Evil ran at the simple mention of Jesus' name.

Few of us will be called to give away everything we have. But God can grow a spirit of generosity and freedom in us as we take steps to rely less on our money, possessions and earthly securities.

Practical steps: During this Lent period consider:

- Fasting from a particular treat (takeaway coffees, buying new clothes, cinema trips etc.) and giving the money you save to a good cause.
- Clearing out cupboards of things you rarely use, and giving them away to other people or charity shops.
- Pausing for a month before making any large purchases, to consider whether you really need it.
- Prayerfully reviewing your regular giving to your church and other charities.
- Secretly supporting a friend or family member with an anonymous gift.

Pray and ask God to help you as you take your steps.

Third Week

A SORROWFUL JOURNEY

"Crying is better than laughing.
It blotches the face but it scours the heart."
(Ecclesiasties 7:3, MSG)

3.1 - SORROWFUL PSALM

"You have put me in the lowest pit, in the darkest depths." (Psalm 88:6)

Read: Psalm 88

Reflect: Think about these questions in relation to the psalm -

- Are there phrases in this psalm which offend you? Which ones, and why?
- Why do you think a text like this is included in the Bible? Do you think that it makes a difference that these emotions are expressed towards God?
- Have you ever felt any of these emotions which the psalmist expresses? Or do you feel that any of the phrases relate to your situation at the moment?
- Do you know anyone who expresses these kinds of emotions? Perhaps pause and pray for them now.

Create: Having reflected, rewrite the whole passage, or part of it, in your own words. Be as honest as you like and use a writing style that feels right to you.

3.2 - HOW LONG?

"They called out in a loud voice, 'How long, Sovereign Lord?'" (Revelation 6:10)

Read: Revelation 6:9-11

"Are we there yet?" is a familiar cry from children in backseats across the world. You might even remember being that child yourself: the uncomfortable seatbelt cutting into your shoulder; the dull, grey view of concrete and lampposts outside the window; perhaps an urge to use a bathroom, a rumble of hunger in your stomach, or an annoying sibling tormenting you from the next seat along. "Please, Mum! Please, Dad! Are we there yet?!"

Sometimes we get a similar feeling as adults. We experience the relentless boredom of the everyday. We might take the same route to work each morning, or rehearse the same daily routine. We can feel that conversations, chores and meals are set on repeat. Isn't there more to life than this?

Or we might well get a similarly uncomfortable feeling watching the news. Like the child who feels powerless to do anything about their confinement in the backseat, we watch the spiralling crises in the world. We are unable to do anything about the horrors of migrants dying at sea or ancient cities being razed to the ground by terrorists. All we can do is cry out, like the child: "how long?".

Reflect: What in your life causes you to cry out "how long?"

_____

_____

_____

_____

_____

_____

_____

_____

_____

Although we might think that we are merely whining when we shout "how long?" towards the TV or computer screen, we are, in fact, using an ancient Biblical prayer. It is not one which we often use at church, perhaps because it is a bit difficult: it has a messy unfinished element to it. It is hard to pray it and then finish with a resounding and confident "Amen." And yet it is a very common prayer for the psalmists and the Old Testament prophets.

In our passage today, we also find it in the New Testament, right towards the end of God's great story. We may think of martyrdom as a thing of the past. We remember the early Christians meeting death at the hands of gladiators in Rome, or old missionaries meeting gruesome fates in far-off lands. However, even the most conservative estimate puts the amount of Christians martyred for their faith today at 10,000 deaths per year. These souls are added each year to the great crowd of martyrs in the heavenly throne room, crying out: "how long?"

This prayer receives an answer in the next verse, but it is perhaps not the answer we want. They are not given an exact time in days and hours and minutes until the evildoers will be punished. Instead, the Lord asks them just to wait a little longer; there is more work to be done.

The child in the backseat is not looking for a technical answer; they are not looking for number of miles, traffic volume and road conditions. They are mostly registering their displeasure at the situation, and in the best case scenario they receive some loving attention from a parent in the front seat.

It is okay to cry "how long?" to God as we watch the news or hear of a friend who's fallen ill. It is okay to whisper or shout "how long?" for your own situations. God wants us to express our complaints to him. He may not immediately solve the issue at hand, but as a loving Father he will turn to us and give us his full attention.

Pray: Spend a few moments calling out your "how long?" prayers to God. However you feel, know that he hears, and that he is with you.

3.3 - CRYING IN THE DESERT

"She went on her way and wandered in the desert... And as she sat there, she began to sob."
(Genesis 21:14,16)

Read: Genesis 21:14-21

Sometimes we choose a wilderness experience, maybe by fasting or simplifying our lives somehow. We sense that in the barrenness of wilderness we can seek God and hear from him more clearly. In contrast, some of us are thrown into wilderness, not by our own doing, but by the sinful acts of others. These times are hard to come to terms with.

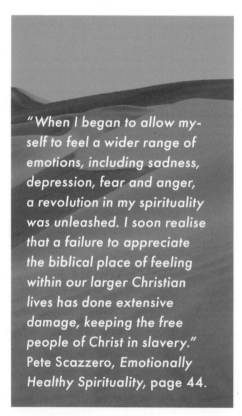

"When I began to allow myself to feel a wider range of emotions, including sadness, depression, fear and anger, a revolution in my spirituality was unleashed. I soon realise that a failure to appreciate the biblical place of feeling within our larger Christian lives has done extensive damage, keeping the free people of Christ in slavery." Pete Scazzero, *Emotionally Healthy Spirituality*, page 44.

I (Sara) find this story of Hagar and Ishmael difficult, because it makes me feel angry with Abraham and Sarah. In some ways, these are the kinds of stories that show the Bible to be a truthful retelling rather than a fairytale. The heroes of our faith are not presented as perfect, far from it. They can be scheming and cruel, like they seem to be in this story, and we learn that even heroes have the potential to sin spectacularly.

The other reason I find this story hard to read is because it involves a suffering child. It paints a heartbreaking picture of a dehydrated teenage boy weeping under a bush in the desert, and a mother who cannot cope with seeing her own child die.

Interestingly, the story includes an answer from God, without there having been a spelled-out prayer. We do not read that Hagar falls on her knees and cries out to God for help. All we know is that she begins to sob, and we also know from the angel's response in verse 17 that Ishmael has been crying.

Could it be that the very emotions we express are prayers before God? Could it be that the presence or absence of an "amen" contributes little to the efficacy of our prayers? I come from a large family and we have an ongoing, but light-hearted feud about whether to end prayers with "amen" or "in Jesus' name, amen." My uncle and half my cousins take my late Grandmother's side and end prayers in the latter way, whereas another aunt's family does not. It always leads to giggles when we say grace during a family gathering. Theoretically we know that these are not the reasons why God hears our prayers, but in practice, and in particularly within corporate worship, many of us can focus on the correctness of our words and ignore other factors.

Pray: We want to invite you to pray using your emotions, like Hagar and Ishmael. Make your words as few as possible. Instead try to express the emotions which arise as consider different things.

1. Make yourself comfortable, and then sit in silence for two minutes. As you do so, note down any thoughts or situations which come to your mind. These might be personal or something in the wider world.

2. What have you jotted down? How do you feel about each of those things? Take the time to allow yourself to really feel the sensations. Do not try to push them down, rationalise or sanitise them. If it helps, write them down.

3. Turn these emotions towards God, with no more than a sense of "God I feel this _____". Allow yourself to sit in his presence with these emotions.

4. Know that "God heard the boy crying" (v. 17) and he will also hear you.

3.4 - MAN OF SORROWS

"As he approached Jerusalem and saw the city, he wept over it" (Luke 19:41)

Read: Luke 13:34-35, 19:41-44

If there is one emotion that comes across when we read of Jesus in the New Testament, it is sorrow. We read of his joy (Luke 10:21) and anger (Mark 3:5). But grief was so central to Jesus' experience that Isaiah spoke of him as a "man of sorrows" (Isa. 53:3)

Today's passages focus on the sorrow he felt over Jerusalem. Jesus shows an incredible capacity for empathy, especially as some of those he was mourning were the same people who were about to kill him in the cruellest way.

I (Sara) love the way Jesus uses maternal language in Luke 13:34. Like a mum, who wants to pull her babies close to her, protecting them from all harm, so Jesus wants to hold the people of Jerusalem close to him. Anyone who has ever cared for someone vulnerable will recognise this desire. Jesus is full of sorrow because they were not willing to come close. I sense a heartbreak here, like a parent rejected by their own child.

In chapter 19, verse 41, Jesus goes one step further and weeps audibly for Jerusalem. He knew the suffering coming to the people of the city, and it caused him to cry with grief, in public.

Can you relate to Jesus here? Or are you more likely to keep these kinds of emotions inside you? We often feel so overwhelmed by all the atrocities of the world, that we end up with compassion-fatigue, unable to feel anything at all.

Reflect: When did you last allow your heart to feel sorrow over a situation in your town, your country or the world at large? Do you struggle to express this?

One cause of this struggle for Christians is because our art and music can sometimes be very "neat", full of positive major chords, bright sunshine and quick resolutions. Pete Greig has written:

> "Where, I wonder, is the mystery and the mess of biblical spirituality? What place is there in our happy-clappy culture for the disturbing message of books such as Ecclesiastes, Lamentations and Job? Where are the moments in both our private and public meetings with God when the major key turns to the minor, when the soft rock anthems pay respect to the blues, and when those top melodies of pop praise finally give way to the scattered logic of jazz?"
> Pete Greig, *God on Mute*, pages 101-102.

Practical steps: Can you find some honest, dark, unresolved music or art to help you enter into the emotions of lament? Or can you create some of your own? One of our attempts is the song "We have come". You can listen to it and watch a video here: **engageworship.org/we-have-come**

It is entirely right and healthy to grieve. However, the Apostle Paul reminds us that we "do not grieve like the rest of mankind, who have no hope." (1 Thess. 4:13) We can mourn with Jesus and we can also be comforted by him. Isaiah continues his description of the coming Messiah:

> "Surely he took up our infirmities and carried our sorrows." (Isa. 53:4a)

Pray: Today, let us allow ourselves to feel some of God's sorrow over the world. Express your grief to Jesus and hand it over to the one who carried your sorrows, placing your hope in him.

3.5 - REMEMBERING IN THE DESERT

"My whole being longs for you, in a dry and parched land" (Psalm 63:1)

Read: Psalm 63

If you've ever fasted or dieted you will know that when you are hungry, everything reminds you of food! The smell of an open fire might make you think of smoked sausages, or the fragrance of coffee might remind you of the cake you want to eat alongside it. We get the feeling that David might have been hungry in the desert:

> "... my soul thirsts for you..." (v. 1)
> "My soul will be satisfied as with the richest of foods..." (v. 5)
> "They [the enemies] will become food for jackals..." (v. 10)

More to the point, his hunger, thirst and solitude in the wilderness seem to have driven him to remind himself of God. "I have seen you in the sanctuary...", David recalls, and "...on my bed I remember you; I think of you through the watches of the night..." (v. 2, 6)

When we are in the wilderness, we too need to remind ourselves to remember God. If we don't, we risk being drawn into a downward spiral of self-pity. It is especially important to remember the last time God provided help. "Because you are my help, I sing in the shadows of your wings..." David recalls poetically.

Spend some time today remembering God. Use the list below to write down things that you want to remember about his character and the way he has previously acted in your life. If you are in the middle of a wilderness right now this could be a difficult exercise, and you may need to dive into the Bible to find truths about God which you may not feel at the moment.

I'm remembering that God...	
1.	4.
2.	5.
3.	6.
	7.

Fourth Week

A SACRIFICIAL JOURNEY

"Do good and share with others, for with such sacrifices God is pleased"
(Hebrews 13:16)

4.1 - JESUS' SACRIFICE

"My God, my God, why have you forsaken me?" (Matthew 27:46)

Read: Matthew 27:45-53

Lent is the season leading up to "Holy Week" when we remember Jesus' last supper, betrayal, trial and crucifixion. For many of us the story is almost too familiar. We have read it so many times, sung about it in hundreds of songs, and seen countless images of the cross or crucifixion. It is important to ask God to give us a fresh glimpse of what Jesus has done for us.

For me (Sam), a fresh experience of the crucifixion came from listening to a recording of composer James MacMillan's "Seven Last Words From The Cross". This discordant, uncomfortable, visceral work for choir and strings sets Jesus' final words as he hung on the cross. If you can, find a recording of it and spend some time experiencing it for yourself.

One of the most striking sections of the piece is the setting of Jesus' cry:

"'Eli, Eli, lema sabachthani?' (which means 'My God, my God, why have you forsaken me?')" (Matt. 27:46)

The word "forsaken" means "abandoned" or "deserted". It describes the wilderness experience of Israel, and the wilderness we all feel from time to time. Jesus is taking upon himself all the laments of Israel through the ages, quoting the desperate lament of Psalm 22 in his moment of deepest despair (read Psalm 22:1-18 for yourself).

Reflect: have you ever felt forsaken, abandoned or deserted? How does it feel to know that Jesus experienced the most extreme version of that?

Jesus was fully human, entirely identifying with our brokenness. But we miss the full implications of this picture if we do not remember that he was also fully *God*, eternally the second person of the Trinity. What must it have felt like for that everlasting relationship to be broken, cut off, "God-forsaken"? Theologian Tom Wright comments:

> "... the whole point of the cross is that there the weight of the world's evil really did converge on Jesus, blotting out the sunlight of God's love as surely as the light of day was blotted out for three hours... the sin of the 'many', which he is bearing, has for the first and only time in his experience caused a cloud to come between him and the father he loved" Tom Wright, *Matthew for Everyone*, page 190.

This week, as we consider the "sacrifice" of wilderness worship, let us begin by kneeling at the cross. Here Jesus makes the ultimate, once-for-all sacrifice for us. He deals with every consequence of our sin, our shame, our wilderness.

Pray: Make this prayer your own:

Jesus, God-forsaken God,
I kneel at your cross in wonder.
Perfect love, perfect sacrifice,
poured out for your Father's glory,
for the sake of the world, and even for me.
May I live in the light of this wonderful cross. Amen.

4.2 - DIFFERENT KINDS OF SACRIFICE

"... continually offer to God a sacrifice of praise" (Hebrews 13:15)

Read: Hebrews 13:11-16

What makes us "right with God"? Is it doing, good works; being "sacrificial" in our life and giving or performing the right religious ceremonies? Whoever wrote the letter to the Hebrews is at pains to point out that *only Jesus' sacrifice* can make us right with God. Yesterday's reflection reminded us that, on the cross, Jesus took the full "God-forsakenness" that separates us from God. Our salvation is a free gift: pre-paid, no strings attached.

So what does "sacrifice" mean for us as Christians? Perhaps this famous quote from *Mere Christianity* by C.S. Lewis can help:

"It is like a small child going to his father and saying, 'Daddy, give me sixpence to buy you a birthday present.' Of course, the father does, and he is pleased with the child's present. It is all very nice and proper, but only an idiot would think that the father is sixpence to the good on the transaction."

Any gift we give back to God, any "sacrifice", is only made possible by the grace of God in the first place. In Hebrews 13:15-16 the writer shows us how we can respond to the grace of God. Our own sacrifices, which we are encouraged to bring, are not in order to make ourselves holy and right with God, but instead are a grateful response to what Christ has already done.

WORSHIP IN THE WILDERNESS

What is a right response to offer for this gift of life? Firstly, we are told to offer a "sacrifice of praise", "fruit of lips that openly profess his name". We are to praise God, proclaim who he is and what he has done for us, bringing glory to him by testifying about him. And here, perhaps, some churches might stop reading: after all, they have good Sunday worship and send their church members on "Telling your testimony in five easy steps" courses. Surely, their sacrifice is complete?

"Not so quick!" says the writer to the Hebrews, who adds an "and" here:

> "And do not forget to do good and to share with others, for with such sacrifices God is pleased." (v. 16)

It turns out that the sacrifice which we are to offer as a grateful response is two-fold: Praise him with words, but also with good deeds. Not good deeds to earn God's favour: instead, an overflow of the kindness God has shown to you. We respond with our lips and our lifestyles.

Spend some time thinking about your own response to Christ's sacrifice for you - do you tend to fall into mostly speaking about Jesus, or mostly acting for Jesus? Reflect in the columns below what you already offer to Christ and think about how you can balance your response today and in the future:

"fruit of my lips"	"doing good and sharing"

4.3 - FROM SORROW TO SACRIFICE

"He withdrew by boat privately to a solitary place. Hearing of this, the crowds followed him..." (Matt 10:13)

Read: Matthew 14:10, 13-21

How do you respond when you are under intense pressure? Do you try to forget about the stress using outward things - a packed leisure schedule, shopping, food or alcohol, escapist film or TV? Or do you close yourself off to the world and sulk in isolation?

Reflect: Note your past responses to stressful events here:

_____

_____

_____

_____

Jesus experienced many stressful events in his short life, but the death of John the Baptist must have hit him especially hard. His cousin and friend, perhaps the person who understood him most, was suddenly gone. The brutal fashion in which John's life had been cut short must have given Jesus pause for thought as well about the likely outcome of his own ministry. If Herod could chop someone's head off on a whim, what else was he capable of?

Jesus' response to this tragic event was to take himself away by boat, somewhere to grieve in private; into the wilderness. Even here, however, he was not left alone, but a large crowd had worked out where he was heading and followed on foot.

If this had been me, to be brutally honest, I (Sara) would have had some sort of breakdown at this point. If I do not get solitude to recharge after stressful events, I suffer (and so does everyone around me). Jesus, however, seems to have greater reserves of patience, generosity, compassion and grace than I will ever come close to.

Instead of telling people to go away, or picking up his oars to row away somewhere different, Jesus "... had compassion on them and healed those who were ill." He then stayed with the crowd all day until late, and miraculously fed the thousands of people there with someone's packed lunch.

Jesus is an inspiration of sacrificial giving here - even in the midst of his own private sorrow, he has compassion on those who are suffering, and keeps on giving of himself.

Now, we are not Jesus. God knows our limits. We need to be wise and not keep giving of ourselves until we reach burn-out. It is a false belief that the responsibility for the salvation of the world somehow rests on our shoulders. It does not - the only saviour of the world is God.

I do, however, draw great comfort from how Jesus partners with his disciples in this story. It was Jesus who made the greatest sacrifice here; missing out on solitude, by healing and teaching and feeding until late. But someone else also brought their own sacrifice. Sure, it was not very big; only five loaves of bread and two fish, but still, it was theirs. Giving it to Jesus may have meant having no food that day - whoever offered it had no way of knowing how it was going to turn out.

This small sacrifice led to a great act of kindness and generosity: the feeding of thousands of hungry people. Will you dare to bring a small sacrifice to Jesus today, and trust him to do something great with it?

Pray: Make this prayer your own:

Jesus, I feel I have so little in the face of the world's needs.
So little time, resources, compassion and energy.
There are times when I am overwhelmed
by my emotions and with the needs around me.
But you have all the resources, compassion and energy.
Help me to bring my bread and fish, my small contribution,
trusting you will multiply it and use it for your glory. Amen.

4.4 - SIMPLE ACTS OF KINDNESS

"... faith by itself, if it is not accompanied by action, is dead." (James 2:17)

The last two days' texts have both emphasised our calling not just to talk about our faith, but to actually live it out in physical, sacrificial ways. Hebrews 13:16 told us to remember to do good to others. In the story in Matthew 14, we take courage that those small acts of goodness can be multiplied when in the hands of Jesus.

Today, why not spend some time asking God how he would have you partner with him in a small act of goodness or kindness? Perhaps you will receive a clear answer from God; a situation might pop into your mind. Or maybe there is already someone or something around you that you've been concerned about lately. A lonely person who would appreciate a visit, rubbish which needs clearing in a park, a new mum who could do with a hot meal delivered, a colleague who could use some help at work, or anything else you might think of. Use the table below to prayerfully plan your act of kindness:

Act of kindness:	
Where?	
When?	
Tick when done:	
Write a prayer that God would multiply this act:	

4.5 - FRAGRANT SACRIFICES

"... a fragrant offering, an acceptable sacrifice, pleasing to God." (Philippians 4:18)

Read: Philippians 4:10-19

In his letter to the church in Philippi, Paul expresses thanks for the gifts the church had recently sent him. He calls them "a fragrant offering, an acceptable sacrifice, pleasing to God." The opposite of a fragrant offering - a stinky one, if you will - can be seen if you dip into the Old Testament prophets. For example, Amos expresses God's distaste for sacrifices offered to him when they are not accompanied by justice (Amos 5:21-24).

Reflect: What is your favourite smell? Is it a particular flower, or perhaps a food item? Are these fragrances related to particular memories of yours?

What is your least favourite smell? What kinds of stink make your toes curl?

Confess: Now, using the imagination you have just engaged when thinking about smells, think about your own worship offerings to God. Think about the worship offerings you sometimes bring, which are perhaps self-seeking, or lack care for the least. Imagine that they stink in the worst way possible. Spend some time saying sorry for the ways you have brought these before God.

The good news is, despite the fact that all of our motives will be mixed and our worship unworthy, Jesus takes it, cleans it up and offers it to the Father. Receive his forgiveness, and his empowering to bring more "fragrant offerings" in the future.

Fifth Week

A TRUTH-SPEAKING JOURNEY

"But the word of our God stands forever...
Shout it louder, O Jerusalem"
(Isaiah 40:8-9)

5.1 - REMEMBERING THE TRUTH

"Let the one who is wise heed these things and ponder the loving deeds of the Lord." (Psalm 107:43)

Part of knowing and speaking God's truth involves having a good memory. When we are in our darkest moments, we may say to ourselves: "Nothing good has ever happened to me. God has never answered my prayers. I have always been this miserable." When we feel in a better place, we recognise these words as untruth. This is why it's so important to record God's actions in our lives, because we forget so quickly!

Read: Psalm 107. This is a long, poetic list of what God has done in the life of Israel, nicely summed up in verse 41: "He lifted the needy out of their affliction".

Create: Try to rewrite Psalm 107, or parts of it, in your own words, using your own experience. Describe some events in your life and how God has acted. You could also include other people's experiences. People around you - do they have testimony of God breaking into their lives which you can add to your psalm?

_____

_____

_____

_____

_____

_____

_____

_____

_____

At the beginning of the psalm the poet writes: "Let the redeemed of the Lord tell their story" (v. 2). This is _your_ story, commit it to memory and remember it in darker times. And once you have thought about it, and remembered all the good things God has done, you can feel confident in speaking it out.

5.2 - LIFT UP YOUR VOICE

"Lift up your voice with a shout, lift it up, do not be afraid" (Isaiah 40:9)

Read: Isaiah 40:3-11

Do you ever feel like you lack a "voice"? Who will listen if you speak out? Politicians, business leaders and celebrities have a platform to speak from, but what about us?

Reflect: What are your experiences of trying to use your voice to speak the truth?

_____

_____

_____

_____

_____

_____

Our passage today is part of a prophecy which the New Testament interprets as pointing towards John the Baptist. He was the one who was called to prepare the way for the Lord (compare Isaiah 40:3 and Matthew 3:3). Although we are not John, in some ways our task is similar to his. Just like John the Baptist, we are not called to try to be the Messiah, but instead to prepare the way in people's hearts for him, and to speak out his truth.

When the prophet in Isaiah 40 is told to "cry out", he replies by asking: "What shall I cry?" (v. 6) Perhaps this rings true for you? Perhaps you want to be like John the Baptist, you want to speak out the truth and use your voice for God, but you don't know what to say?

The next part of the passage gives us some helpful direction. Human beings and their glory are momentary, we are told, like the wildflowers: there one day and gone the next. Politicians come and go. People get rich, but they still pass away, or lose their fortune. People get famous, but they still don't last forever, or they have a disastrous fall from grace. Human glory is momentary.

In comparison, we are told that "the word of our God stands forever" (v. 8). Here are words to rely on, to draw inspiration from, to be encouraged by and to speak out.

This does not mean that everyone is called to stand on street corners and preach three-point sermons! Speaking God's word, speaking his truth, can mean explaining the gospel in a winsome way. But it can also mean adding your name to a campaign against an injustice, or gently telling the ladies at the coffee mornings that you do not want to gossip, or stopping sexist talk in its tracks when you are with your friends in the pub.

And speaking God's word is not all about protesting the negatives, it is also about peppering the conversations around you with God's life-affirming, positive truths. Rather than be seen as kill-joys, we can be true joy bringers. Let people know that they are loved and precious for who they are, highlight the good which national or local leaders do, point out when you see someone doing something kind or helpful.

Reflect: Can you think of a situation where you might speak God's truth in the upcoming days?

Pray: Make this prayer your own:

Word of God, may my speech be full of your truth,
your grace and your righteousness.
Guide my words and give me boldness
to speak what is on your heart
in each situation. Amen.

5.3 - WORDS OF ETERNAL LIFE

"The words I have spoken to you – they are full of the Spirit and life." (John 6:63)

Read: John 6:60-69

Jesus, like the rest of us, experienced varying degrees of popularity. Human beings are fickle, as you have probably experienced for yourself. A friend of mine was telling me (Sara) the other day how her daughter all of a sudden became very popular when rumours spread of her impending, and exciting, birthday party. Once the invites had gone out, however, those without the coveted cards went back to ignoring her.

Jesus was popular when he came across as the powerful Messiah the people had been waiting for. For example, they liked him a lot after his miraculous healings, and celebrated him at the triumphant entry into Jerusalem which we remember on Palm Sunday. At other times, the crowds abandoned him and left him lonely and isolated.

John 6 starts with Jesus flying high in the approval ratings. Everyone loves food, and a miraculous feeding of thousands would always be a popular move. Later on, however, as Jesus makes some rather grand claims about himself, the religious leaders become a bit nervous. Once it starts to sound like Jesus is advocating cannibalism, everyone simply slips away. Rather than having to get their heads around what Jesus might mean, most people in the crowd see which way the wind is blowing and follow their peers to the next popular celebrity.

Some, however, are loyal. When queried about this by Jesus, Peter comes out with his famous creed:

> "Lord, to whom shall we go? You have the words of eternal life. We have come to believe and to know that you are the Holy One of God." (vs. 68-69)

There is such beauty in these simple words of trust. These are the words of someone who has spent long enough with Jesus to know that however hard his latest teaching might be, the very source of life is within him and so going elsewhere would be foolish indeed.

I don't know if you've had this experience, but sometimes when we speak the truth our popularity drops too. However gently you may challenge your friend's habit of spreading rumours, or however carefully you may put your reasons for not attending a questionably themed office party, those around you may still hear it as criticism. And nobody likes being criticised!

Reflect: Are there times when you've tried to speak out God's truth, but it has made you unpopular or rejected?

For Jesus, speaking the truth was not a popularity contest. His words were "full of the Spirit and life", "words of eternal life." More than wise sayings or religious slogans, these words have transformative, divine power, if we have "ears to hear".

Practical steps: Spend some time in the words of Jesus today. This could involve:

- Choose one passage of Jesus' words, and commit it to memory.
- Write a tune (or find an existing tune) to set a section of Jesus' teaching, so that you remember it and carry it around with you.
- Listen to an audio Bible version of Jesus' teaching.
- Create a poster with a verse from the gospels and hang it somewhere you will see it regularly.

None of these things are "ends in themselves": the point is to soak yourself in the words of Jesus, and allow the Holy Spirit to take them from your head to your heart.

5.4 - TRUTH AGAINST TEMPTATION

"Take... the sword of the Spirit, which is the word of God" (Ephesians 6:17)

Read: Luke 4:1-13

In Ephesians 6, when Paul writes about the spiritual armour we are to dress ourselves in for protection against evil, he mentions only one weapon. This is the "... sword of the Spirit, which is the word of God." (Eph. 6:17) If you want to learn how to use this particular item in your armoury, the best sword fighting lesson can be found in the story of Jesus' forty days in the wilderness.

When you are tempted to sin, no doubt the temptations are custom made for you. The devil knows which buttons to press and when you are at your weakest. Before temptation hits, it can be useful to fill up our armoury with the swords which will be powerful in our particular contexts. You can see that we have started a table below - spend some time prayerfully thinking of Bible texts which can counter your own temptations.

Temptation	Sword of the Spirit verse
Break his fast	Deuteronomy 8:3: "Man shall not live on bread alone."
Take the easy route to power & authority	Deuteronomy 6:13: "Worship the Lord your God and serve him only."
Test God, show off	Deuteronomy 6:16: "Do not put the Lord your God to the test."

5.5 - SPEAK TO THE DRY BONES

"I prophesied as he commanded me, and breath entered them; they came to life and stood up on their feet" (Ezekiel 37:10)

Read: Ezekiel 37:1-14

The people in Ezekiel's time were sure that their situation was hopeless, helpless, dead-and-rotten. God showed them that by his Word and his Spirit he could bring the dead back to life, restoring an entire people.

Reflect: What places and people in your town, your country, this planet, do you feel a sense of hopelessness about? What seems dead-and-rotten?

_____

_____

_____

_____

Pray: Ask God to give you his words of truth and life for those situations. Pray them - ideally aloud and confidently - over those people and places. Declare them in the power of God's Spirit and with confidence in his Word.

These dry bones get everywhere. But so does the breath of God.

Palm Sunday

A SURPRISING JOURNEY

"The desert and the parched land will be glad; the wilderness will rejoice and blossom"
(Isaiah 35:1)